Smart Animals

SEA LIONS

by Margaret Fetty

Consultant: Jenny Montague
Assistant Curator of Marine Mammals
New England Aquarium
Boston, MA

BEARPORT
PUBLISHING

New York, New York

Credits

Cover and Title Page, © istockphoto, Werner Stoffberg; 4, © Brien Aho / U.S. Navy / Newscom; 5, © Bob Houlihan / U.S. Navy / Newscom; 6, © Bob Houlihan / U.S. Navy / Newscom; 7, © SHNS photo courtesy U.S. Navy / NewsCom; 8, © Jeffrey L. Rotman / CORBIS; 9, © Jeffrey L. Rotman / CORBIS; 10, © Courtesy of Dr. Ronald J. Schusterman, Long Marine Laboratory, Institute of Marine Sciences at University of California Santa Cruz; 11, © Courtesy of Dr. Ronald J. Schusterman, Long Marine Laboratory, Institute of Marine Sciences at University of California Santa Cruz; 12, © Courtesy of Dr. Ronald J. Schusterman, Long Marine Laboratory, Institute of Marine Sciences at University of California Santa Cruz; 13, © Courtesy of Dr. Ronald J. Schusterman, Long Marine Laboratory, Institute of Marine Sciences at University of California Santa Cruz; 14, © Dave Herring; 15, © Frans Lanting / Minden Pictures; 16, © SeaPics.com; 17, © John Francis / CORBIS; 18, © Gregory Ochocki / Photo Researchers Inc.; 19, © Kelvin Aitken / Peter Arnold, Inc.; 20, © Diego Lezama Orezzoli / CORBIS; 21, © SeaPics.com; 22, © Kelvin Aitken / Peter Arnold, Inc.; 23, © Kennan Ward / CORBIS; 24, © Mary Ann McDonald / CORBIS; 25, © D. Parer & E. Parer-Cook / AUSCAPE / Minden Pictures; 26, © Brandon D. Cole / CORBIS; 27, © STR / AFP / Getty Images; 28L, © Barbara Von Hoffmann / Animals Animals-Earth Scenes; 28R, © Shane Moore / Animals Animals-Earth Scenes; 29, © New England Aquarium.

Publisher: Kenn Goin
Project Editor: Adam Siegel
Creative Director: Spencer Brinker
Design: Dawn Beard Creative

Library of Congress Cataloging-in-Publication Data

Fetty, Margaret.
  Sea Lions / by Margaret Fetty.
      p. cm. — (Smart animals!)
  Includes bibliographical references (p.   ) and index.
  ISBN-13: 978-1-59716-274-6 (lib. bdg.)
  ISBN-10: 1-59716-274-4 (lib. bdg.)
  ISBN-13: 978-1-59716-302-6 (pbk.)
  ISBN-10: 1-59716-302-3 (pbk.)
  1. Sea lions—Juvenile literature. 2. Sea lions—Psychology—Juvenile literature.
I. Title. II. Series.

  QL737.P63F48 2007
  599.79'75—dc22
                        2006011318

For more information, write to Bearport Publishing Company, Inc., 101 Fifth Avenue, Suite 6R, New York, New York 10003. Printed in the United States of America.

10 9 8 7 6 5 4 3 2 1

Contents

Zak on Guard

Zak swims through the **harbor**. He is searching for enemy divers who are trying to blow up U.S. Navy ships.

Zak listens for clues. He hears the soft sounds of air bubbles floating through the water. They may be coming from a dangerous diver. So Zak goes into action.

▲ **Zak is a 375-pound (170-kg) California sea lion.**

4

First, Zak quietly swims up behind the enemy. He then attaches a clamp to the swimmer's leg. Before the diver knows what has happened, Zak swims away. A rope is connected to the clamp. Sailors can now pull the enemy out of the water and question him.

▲ **Zak leaps onto a boat after training.**

Dolphins and whales, as well as sea lions, have been trained to help the U.S. **military**.

An Intelligent Choice

Since 1975, sea lions like Zak have been trained by the U.S. Navy. They have been taught to guard harbors and carry tools and equipment. They have also been taught to find and **recover** objects lost in oceans and lakes.

▲ Sea lions are trained for about a year and a half before they are ready to work for the Navy.

Sea lions have many skills that make them a good choice for Navy training. These clever **mammals** can see well in deep, dark water. They can hear faraway sounds. They can dive many times without getting tired. Sea lions can also move quickly on land and in water. So they can chase an enemy out of the ocean.

▲ **This sea lion is trained to recover objects lost in the water.**

Sea lions can dive down more than 500 feet (152 m). So it's easy for them to find objects deep in the ocean.

A Whale of a Good Time

The U.S. Navy isn't the only group to discover that sea lions can help humans. Some scientists in California wanted to study whales. However, these giant creatures swim hundreds of feet below the ocean's surface. It's hard for people to dive down that far. Yet deep dives are no problem for sea lions. So scientists began teaching them how to film the whales.

▲ **A sea lion with an underwater video camera on its back**

Beaver was a sea lion trained to swim alongside whales. He wore a **harness** with a camera that would record the animals' movements and sounds. Scientists could then study Beaver's film to learn more about how whales live.

▲ **This sea lion is being trained to use an underwater video camera.**

Whales are used to seeing sea lions swim next to them. So, unlike humans, sea lions can film the huge animals without disturbing them.

A Rocky Language

Sea lions are quick learners. Yet could they be taught to understand a kind of sign language? Ronald Schusterman, a scientist in Santa Cruz, California, wanted to find out. Rocky, a female sea lion, became his first student.

Dr. Schusterman taught Rocky many hand signals. Each one stood for a different object, color, or action. If he made the sign for "ball," Rocky would touch a ball with her nose.

▲ **Ronald Schusterman and Rocky**

Next, Dr. Schusterman taught Rocky to follow two hand signals. After placing up to nine objects in Rocky's pool, he made the signs for "ball" and "tail touch." Rocky put the two signs together. She found the ball and touched it with her tail. Rocky understood the language!

◀ **A trainer giving hand signals to Rocky**

After two years, Rocky understood 20 different hand signals that could be combined in 190 different ways.

A Memory Test

Dr. Schusterman also wondered if sea lions could remember things they had learned long ago. He had worked for many years with a sea lion named Rio. So he decided to test her **long-term memory**.

▲ **Rio**

When Rio was six years old, she had been taught to identify matching pictures. Over the next ten years, however, Rio wasn't asked to use this skill again.

When Rio was 16 years old, Dr. Schusterman wondered if she would still remember how to match pictures. So he put cards in front of her that had different shapes on them. She quickly found the matching pair. Rio hadn't forgotten!

▲ **Rio touches the shape that matches the center picture.**

Rio also learned to tell the difference between numbers and letters.

Out in the Wild

Rio's behavior showed that **captive** sea lions can remember what they learn. This discovery isn't a surprise to scientists who study wild sea lions. They already know these animals remember many things.

California Sea Lions in the Wild

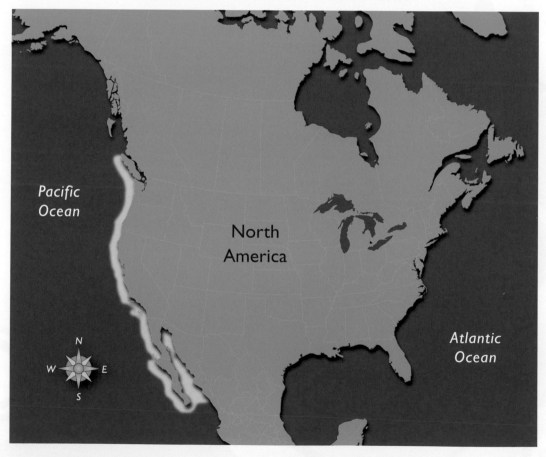

Pacific
Ocean

North
America

Atlantic
Ocean

N
W · E
S

■ Area where California
sea lions live

▲ **There are several kinds of sea lions. Rocky and Rio were California sea lions.**

For example, female sea lions, called **cows**, remember the beaches where they were born. They return there each year to give birth to their babies, called **pups**.

Each male sea lion, known as a **bull**, chooses a part of the beach for himself. This is his **territory**. During the winter, he **migrates** to other places to find food. Yet in the spring he remembers how to find his way back to his old area.

▲ **In the wild, thousands of sea lions live in a group called a colony.**

The sea lion got its name because the male makes a sound like a lion's roar.

Communication

A bull doesn't share his territory. He barks loudly to frighten away other males that try to take his land. He is telling the other sea lions to go away. Being able to **communicate** is a sign of intelligence.

▲ **Bulls fighting with each other**

Communication is also important between mothers and pups. A mother may leave her pup for up to two days to get food. When she returns, there are hundreds of pups on the beach. How does she find her baby?

Each mother has a special bark. The mother makes her call and the pup barks back. The two repeat the calls until they find each other.

▲ **A mother sea lion smells a pup to make sure it is hers.**

A mother sea lion doesn't waste any time training her pup to recognize her voice. She barks straight into a pup's face after it is born.

Skillful Watching

Many smart animals learn how to do things by watching. Sea lion pups don't know how to swim well when they are born. They don't know how to catch fish. So the pups must watch adult sea lions to learn these skills.

▲ **A pup stays in shallow water until it learns to swim.**

At first, a pup just watches its mother swim and dive. When it is about two weeks old, the pup first tries to swim. Within four weeks, it has learned how to be a good swimmer. By the time the sea lion is six months old, it can even catch its own food.

▲ **A sea lion pup usually lives with its mother until it is about one year old.**

Sea lions have a layer of fat called **blubber**, which keeps them warm. Pups can't stay in cold water very long because their blubber is too thin.

Hunting with Whiskers

Pups also learn how to use their whiskers as they grow up. Sometimes the ocean water is dark or muddy. It's hard for the sea lion to see the fish that it wants to catch. So the sea lion uses its whiskers to find **prey**.

▼ **A sea lion pup's whiskers**

If a sea lion's whiskers are facing forward, the animal is probably curious. If the sea lion barks with whiskers forward, the animal may be angry.

A sea lion can sweep its whiskers along the ocean floor. They help the sea lion feel for fish that might be hiding there. The whiskers can also feel the movements in the water made by fish and squid. This information helps the sea lion know where to hunt.

▲ Some sea lions eat about 40 pounds (18 kg) of fish in one day.

Playful Pups

Baby sea lions also learn by playing with other pups. They chase each other across the rocks. They bark at one another. The pups even wrestle and bite each other.

▲ **Sea lion pups at play**

Scientists say playing is a sign of a smart animal. Playful pups are learning adult skills. When male pups wrestle and bite, they are learning how to guard their territory. When baby sea lions bark, they are learning how to communicate with one another.

▲ **Sea lions playfully biting each other**

Male sea lion pups playfully bite and bark to learn how to defend their territories when they become grown bulls.

Emotion in the Ocean

A mother sea lion has one pup each year. She takes very good care of her baby. She spends a full year teaching her pup important skills that will help it survive. A baby sea lion learns how to swim fast to escape from sharks and killer whales.

▲ **A mother taking her pup on a swim**

Sometimes, however, a killer whale or shark sneaks up on a pup. The pup cannot swim fast enough to get away. The mother squeals as she watches the **predator** take her baby. Like other smart animals, sea lions can communicate their feelings.

▲ **A killer whale trying to catch sea lions**

Killer whales and sharks hunt sea lions for food.

Sea Lion Safety

In the past, humans hunted sea lions for their blubber and fur. Today, garbage and oil spills can poison and kill these animals. Some fishermen get angry at sea lions for damaging their nets, so they shoot them.

Steller sea lions living near Alaska are **endangered** because their food supplies are disappearing due to climate changes and increased fishing.

▲ **Steller sea lions**

To protect sea lions, countries have passed laws that make it **illegal** to hunt the animals. In California, the Marine Mammal Center gives medical help to **injured** sea lions. Then they are returned to their **habitat**. If the animals cannot return safely, they are given new homes in zoos or aquariums. These intelligent animals can then get the care, attention—and fish—they deserve from their human friends.

◄ **After being cleaned off from an oil spill, this sea lion is returned to the ocean.**

Just the Facts

California Sea Lion

Steller Sea Lion

	California Sea Lion		Steller Sea Lion
Weight	150–1,000 pounds (68–454 kg)	**Weight**	600–2,200 pounds (272–998 kg)
Length	5–8 feet (1.5–2.4 m)	**Length**	6–11 feet (1.8–3.3 m)
Life Span	20–25 years	**Life Span**	20–25 years
Habitat	from British Columbia to Baja California in Mexico	**Habitat**	California, and from the Arctic to Japan
Food	fish, octopuses, squid	**Food**	fish, octopuses, squid
Predators	killer whales, sharks	**Predators**	killer whales, sharks
Status	not endangered	**Status**	endangered

More Smart Sea Lions

A group of wild sea lions in California has found an easy way to find food. The animals have learned to follow fishing boats and wait for the people to catch fish. Before the fish are reeled in, the sea lions eat the tasty treats right off the hook! About 20 percent of the hooked fish end up in the sea lions' bellies.

At the New England Aquarium in Boston, three sea lions have been taught to paint. Trainer Paul Bradley puts paint on a brush and gives it to one of the sea lions. The sea lion takes the brush in his mouth and makes lines and dots on a canvas. When finished, the hardworking artist gets a fish reward.

▲ **Tyler painting at the New England Aquarium**

Glossary

blubber (BLUH-bur) the fat under a sea lion's skin

bull (BUL) a male sea lion

captive (KAP-tiv) not living in one's natural environment; living with and being cared for by people

communicate (kuh-MYOO-nuh-kate) share information, ideas, feelings, and thoughts

cows (KOUZ) female sea lions

endangered (en-DAYN-jurd) in danger of dying out

habitat (HAB-uh-*tat*) a place in nature where an animal normally lives

harbor (HAR-bur) an area of water where ships can safely stay or unload goods

harness (HAR-niss) a piece of equipment that is strapped to an animal

illegal (i-LEE-guhl) against the law

injured (IN-jurd) hurt

long-term memory (LAWNG-turm MEM-uh-ree) the ability to remember information that was learned long ago

mammals (MAM-uhlz) animals that are warm-blooded, nurse their young with milk, and have hair or fur on their skin

migrates (MYE-grates) moves from one place to another during a particular time of the year

military (MIL-uh-*ter*-ee) having to do with the armed forces

predator (PRED-uh-tur) an animal that hunts other animals for food

prey (PRAY) animals that are hunted or caught for food

pups (PUPS) baby sea lions

recover (ree-KOV-ur) get something back

territory (TER-uh-*tor*-ee) an area of land that belongs to an animal

Bibliography

Page, George. *Inside the Animal Mind: A Groundbreaking Exploration of Animal Intelligence.* New York: Doubleday (1999).

http://slewths.mlml.calstate.edu/slewths.htm

www.nwf.org

www.sandiegozoo.org

www.spawar.navy.mil

Read More

Arnold, Caroline. *Sea Lion.* New York: Morrow Junior Books (1994).

Pichon, Joelle. *The Sea Lion: Ocean Diver.* Watertown, MA: Charlesbridge Publishing (1997).

Shehata, Kat. *San Francisco's Famous Sea Lions.* Cincinnati, OH: Angel Bea Publishing (2002).

Learn More Online

Visit these Web sites to learn more about sea lions:

http://nmml.afsc.noaa.gov/education/pinnipeds/California2.htm

www.lazoo.org/sealionsummer/slinfo.html

www.seaworld.org/animal-info/info-books/california-sea-lion/

Index

About the Author

Margaret Fetty has written numerous children's books. She lives in Austin, Texas, where she enjoys running and biking.